Go

Dave Boyle
Wendy Pitt

CAMBRIDGE
UNIVERSITY PRESS

S · T · E · P

Published by the Press Syndicate of the University of Cambridge
The Pitt Building, Trumpington Street, Cambridge CB2 1RP
40 West 20th Street, New York, NY 10011–4211, USA
10 Stamford Road, Oakleigh, Melbourne 3166, Australia

In association with Staffordshire County Council

© Cambridge University Press 1992

First published 1992

Printed in Great Britain by Scotprint Ltd, Musselburgh

Designed and produced by Gecko Limited, Bicester, Oxon.

A catalogue record of this book is available from the British Library.

ISBN 0 521 40631 5

PICTURE ACKNOWLEDGEMENTS

Anthony Blake Picture Library 6tr, 6bl, 6br.
Christopher Coggins 4, 6tl, 10–11, 23.
English Heritage 25, 26c.
Sally and Richard Greenhill 22br.
Robert Harding Picture Library 6cr, 22tl.
Hutchison Picture Library 22tr.
Kentucky Fried Chicken/Tantrums 14tl.
Last Resort 14br, 21.
Diane Mortimer 26tr.
Zefa Ltd. 14tr.

Picture Research by Linda Proud

NOTICE TO TEACHERS

The contents of this book are in the copyright of Cambridge University Press. Unauthorised copying of any of the pages is not only illegal but also goes against the interests of the authors.

For authorised copying please check that your school has a licence (through the Local Education Authority) from the Copyright Licensing Agency which enables you to copy small parts of the text in limited numbers.

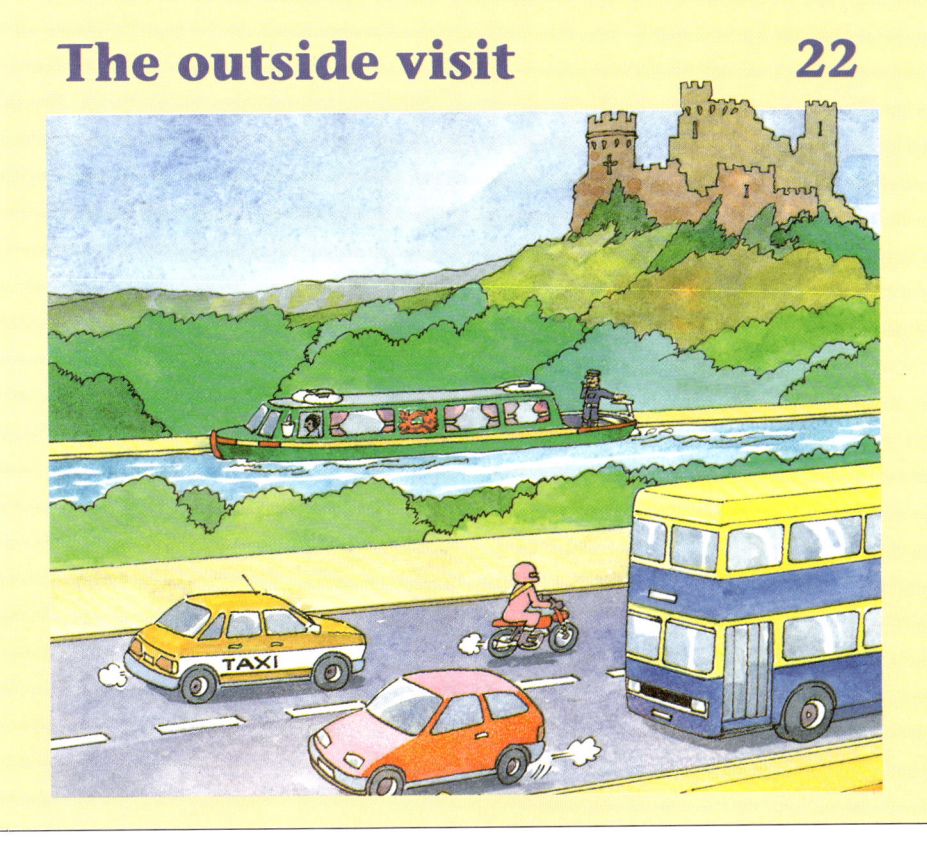

Contents

Eat for health   4

Cash flow   16

The outside visit   22

Eat *for Health*

Talking together

What different kinds of food can you see in the picture?
Have you eaten any of these foods?
What do they taste like?

What food do you enjoy eating?
What food do you not enjoy?

Do you think it matters what food we eat?
Why is this?

Some foods are better for us than others.
Which of the foods in the pictures encourage healthy growth.
What information do you need to find?
Where can you go to do the research?

Discuss these questions with your friends to help you get some ideas.

What different ways of cooking can you think of?
What kinds of food can we cook?
What kinds of food can we eat without cooking?
What happens to food when it is cooked?

Sometimes it is the way that food is prepared that makes it less healthy. Find out which ways of preparing food are better for us than others?

The need

Imagine your class is due to go on a school trip. You could raise money for this by setting up a school tuck shop. It is important to encourage healthy eating by selling healthy food at the tuck shop.

THE RUMBLING TUM TUCKSHOP

Developing your design

You need to find out:
- what you can sell in the tuck shop
- what people are prepared to buy
- how much money they will spend

You also need to think about:
- where your tuck shop is going to be situated
- who will look after the shop
- how you will prepare the food
- hygiene regulations for selling food

Consumer research

After finding out what kinds of food you can sell in the tuck shop you may want to design a survey to find out which of these foods people would buy and how much money they may spend.

Once you know what people want you can make some decisions about the range of goods you will sell in the shop.

A survey will help you to find out who would use the shop and how much they could afford to spend.

• DATA FILE •
Research: data collection and display

Preparing food for a survey

To find out what kinds of foods people want to buy you may need to prepare some for them to eat.

Set up a sterile area and then prepare yourself to work with food.

Prepare the food for your survey.

• D A T A F I L E •

Basic equipment:
for food

Food Preparation:
myself

Conduct your trials.

• DATA FILE •
Research: data collection and display

Set up a production line to produce the food.

· DATA FILE ·
Planning a production line

More ideas

Design a uniform and some equipment for the shop assistants so that they can serve food hygienically and safely.

Design and make bags for customers to carry away their food.

Set up an advertising campaign for the tuck shop.

Design and make covers for your food that will keep it safe from contamination.

Set up a system to make sure that:
- the shop has people serving in it
- the storage area in the shop is kept clean and well organised
- the customers know what there is to buy and how much things cost
- you have a record of how much is being spent on food each week, in the tuck shop

Cash flow

Talking together

Where do people go to borrow money?
How could the money for starting your tuck shop be raised?
Will the Bank or a local Building Society be interested in lending any money to you?
Perhaps there is another person or group of people who would be prepared to lend you some money.
How could you find out who would be willing to help you?

The need

To start off any business you need to raise some money. You can borrow money from many different organisations although they will need to be sure that you can pay the money back.

To start off the tuck shop business you will need money to buy food and equipment.

How will you raise your money?

Developing your design

How are you going to persuade someone to lend you some money?
How much will they charge you to borrow their money?
Can you convince them that the tuck shop will be a success?

What will you sell and where will you sell? What will you buy and from whom?

Who will work for you? Yourself, your class, teacher, family friends.

How you will advertise? Newspaper radio leaflets.

What materials will you need? What specialist rooms, tools or equipment might you need?

Where you will work from? Home, school.

How will you finance yourself? Loan, savings, voluntary contributions.

Think of ways to approach banks, industries, building societies or parents to find out if they will invest money in the tuck shop.

One way to raise money is to sell people a 'share' in your business. Find out what 'shares' are. Could you sell shares in the tuck shop?

Write letters and invitations.
Develop a presentation to persuade the people to invest in your ideas.

- DATA FILE -
Letters and invitations

More ideas

Where can you buy the tuck from? Is there a special place where you can get the tuck wholesale?

The *Outside* visit

Talking together

There are many different things that can be done as part of an outside visit.

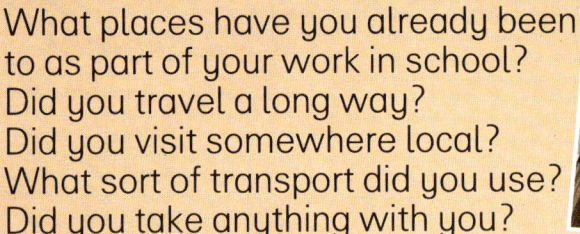

What places have you already been to as part of your work in school?
Did you travel a long way?
Did you visit somewhere local?
What sort of transport did you use?
Did you take anything with you?
What did you do when you got to your destination?
What sort of visit would help your work in school now?

You may have collected souvenirs or taken photographs to remind you of the places you have visited in the past. Use them to make a display of all the places you and your friends have been to.

23

The need

As part of your term's work the class is to go on a visit. Imagine your teacher is leaving all the arrangements for you and the class to organise. You must decide where to go, how to get there and what to do on the day. You have six weeks to organise the visit.

WEEK 1 Where to go?

WEEK 2 How to go?

WEEK 3 Advise parents

WEEK 4 Gather information

WEEK 5 Plan details

WEEK 6 Distribute plan

Developing your design

There are many things to consider when you are organising a group of people to go away together.

Hadrian's Wall was built by the Romans about 1800 years ago. It defended the northern frontier of their empire. Outside it lived the Scots whom they were unable to defeat.

Hadrian's Wall

HOUSESTEADS
CORBRIDGE
CHESTERS

Exploring Roman Northumberland

...on a ridge overlooking the open moorlan[d of] Northumbria, conveys the spirit of the past as well as beauty of the present. It is the starting point for bra[cing] and breathtaking walks along the wall to Steel Rigg to [the] west and Sewingshields to the east.

The fort covers five acres in a characteristic playi[ng] card shape, with a protective wall surrounding the re[-] mains of many buildings. The remains of the granaries, commandant's house, barrack blocks, latrines and gate[-] ways can all be clearly seen, many in a fine state of preservation so that you can see how such buildings were originally constructed and used.

There is a site museum with displays of finds and a model of the fort and civilian settlement.

INFORMATION

OPENING HOURS

Good Friday or 1 April (whichever is earlier) to 30 September:
Open Daily 10 am-6 pm.
1 October to Maundy Thursday or 31 March (whichever is earlier):
Open Daily 10 am-4 pm.

ADMISSION 1991

[Se]nior Citizens, Students and UB40 Holders £1.20. [En]glish Heritage Members free. Special party rates. [...] (½ mile to the south on the main road). Access for [...] site, enquire at Information Centre on main road).

HOW TO GET THERE

[N]orth-east of Bardon Mill on the B6318.
[ ]85 (Newcastle to Carlisle service) to within 2¾ miles.
[8]90 (hail-and-ride service, from mid-July to early [...] een Hexham and Haltwhistle Stations and passing [...]ain: 2¾ miles from Bardon Mill Station.
[...]NY790687. Telephone: (0434) 344363

Where are you going?
Why are you going to this place?
What could you do when you get there?
How much will it cost?
How much can you afford?
How are you going to get there?
What routes can you take?

Where will you go?

What work have you done in class this term?

What work will you be doing at the time of the visit?

What sort of visit would help your work in school?

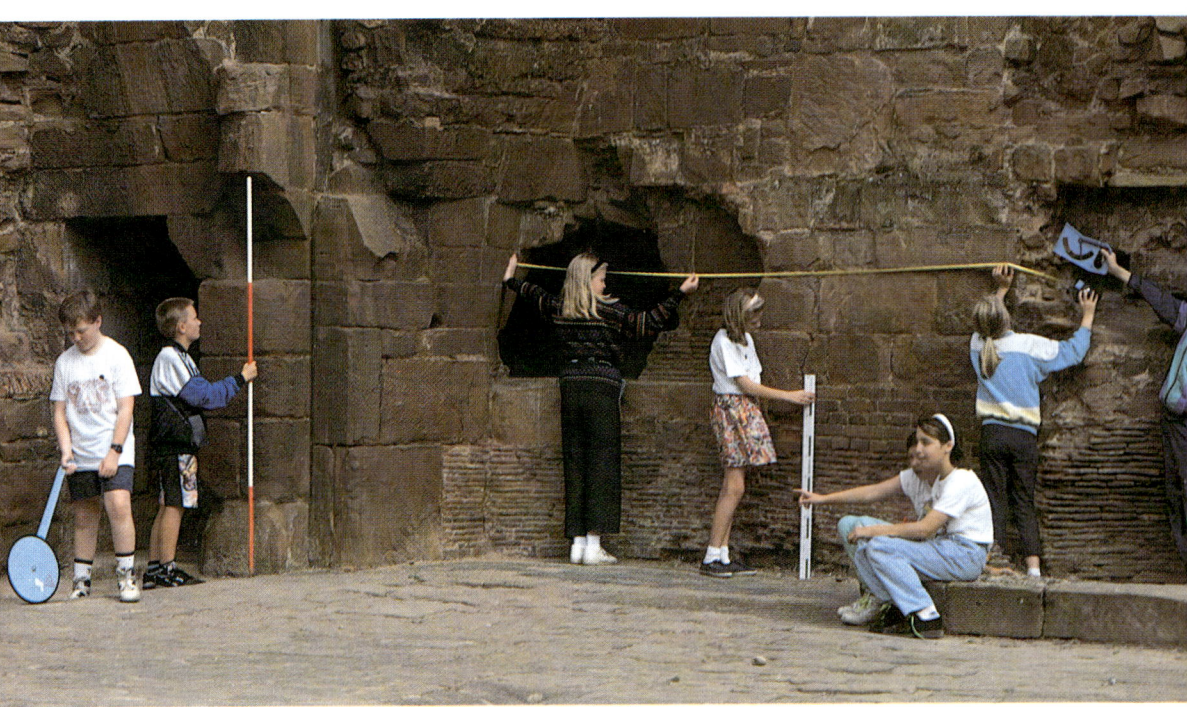

Make a list of places to visit that would help you in your work at school and survey the class to find out which place they would like to visit the most.

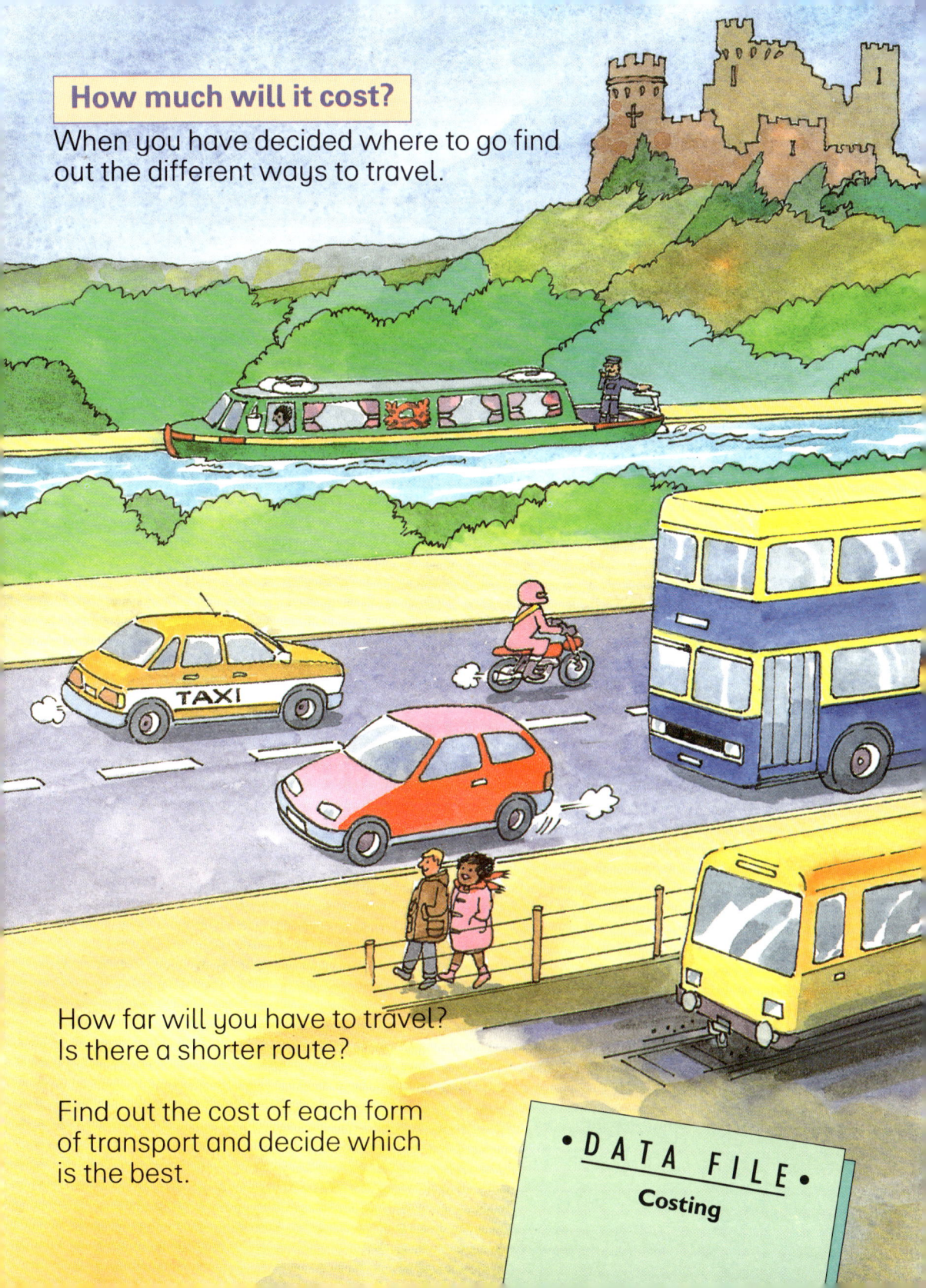

How much will it cost?

When you have decided where to go find out the different ways to travel.

How far will you have to travel? Is there a shorter route?

Find out the cost of each form of transport and decide which is the best.

• D A T A   F I L E •
Costing

On the day

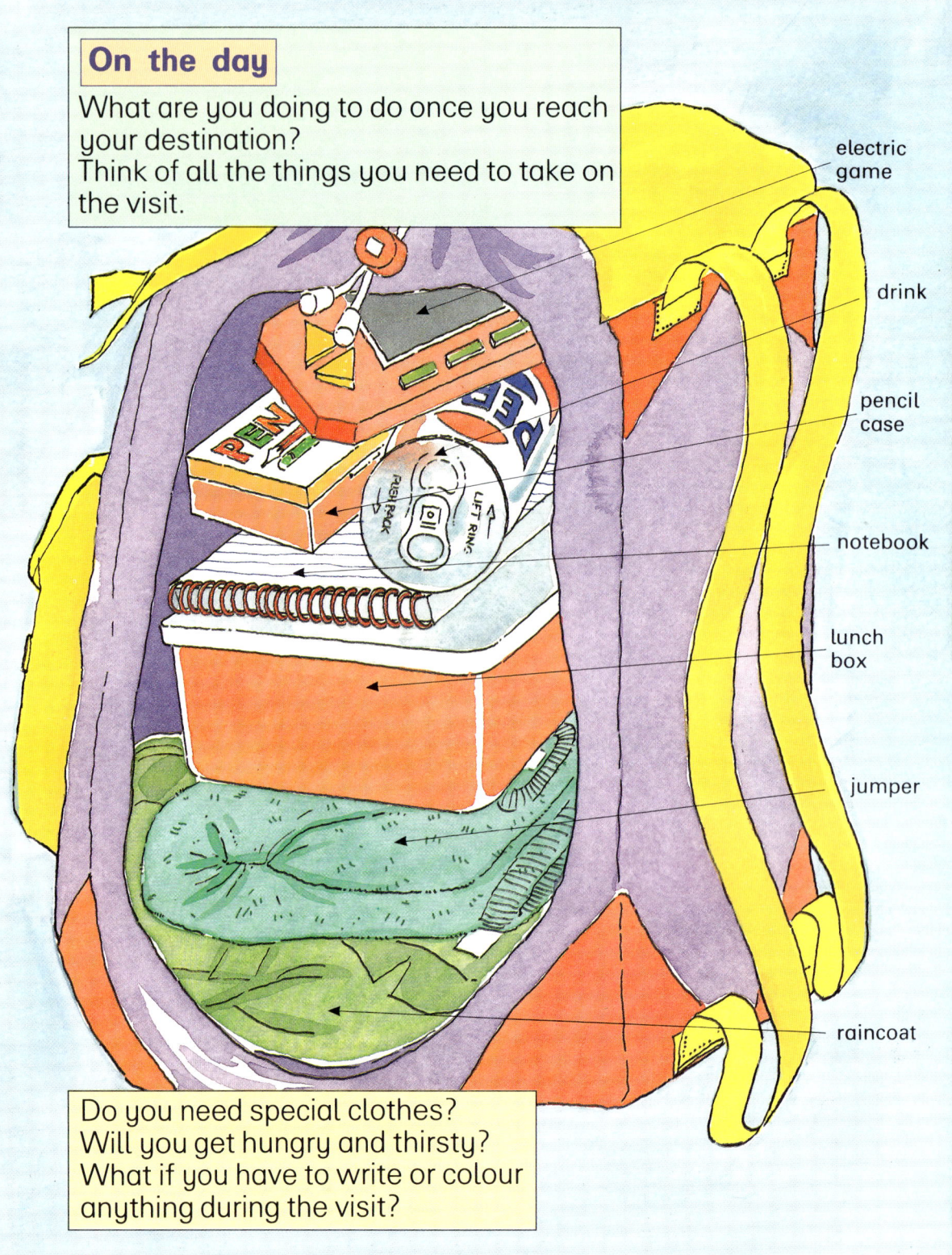

What are you doing to do once you reach your destination?
Think of all the things you need to take on the visit.

electric game

drink

pencil case

notebook

lunch box

jumper

raincoat

Do you need special clothes?
Will you get hungry and thirsty?
What if you have to write or colour anything during the visit?

28

If you need to take food how can you keep it
- cool
- warm
- fresh
- unsquashed?

Plastic box

Vacuum flask

An information leaflet

Design an information leaflet for parents so that they know all the details of the visit.
You may want it to include information about
- food
- drinks
- the time you will leave school
- the time you will arrive home

Visit to Hadrian's Wall

Timetable
Depart school gate 9:00
Arrive Hadrian's Wall 10:00
Depart Hadrian's Wall 15:00
Arrive school gate 16:00

Information
Food: A packed lunch should be brought.
Money: Children should bring a small amount of spending money, for guide books, drinks and snacks.
Clothing: A wind proof coat will be needed. It can be cold and windy on Hadrians Wall.

Our visit
We have been studying the Romans in class this term and our visit to Hadrian's Wall will help everyone to appreciate the skill and engineering achievement of one of the worlds greatest empires. We plan to visit Vindolanda civillian settlements as well as Housesteads Fort.

The leaflet could also have a permission section for parents or guardians to sign.

• DATA FILE •
Uses of Information Technology

Safety

You need to think about the safety of everyone on the visit.

What would happen if someone got lost or needed help?
Will everyone need to know where to meet together at lunchtime or hometime?
What should happen in case of an accident?
Who could help with first aid?

Design a system so that members of the class know what they should do during the day and if they need help.

• **DATA FILE** •
Systems

More ideas

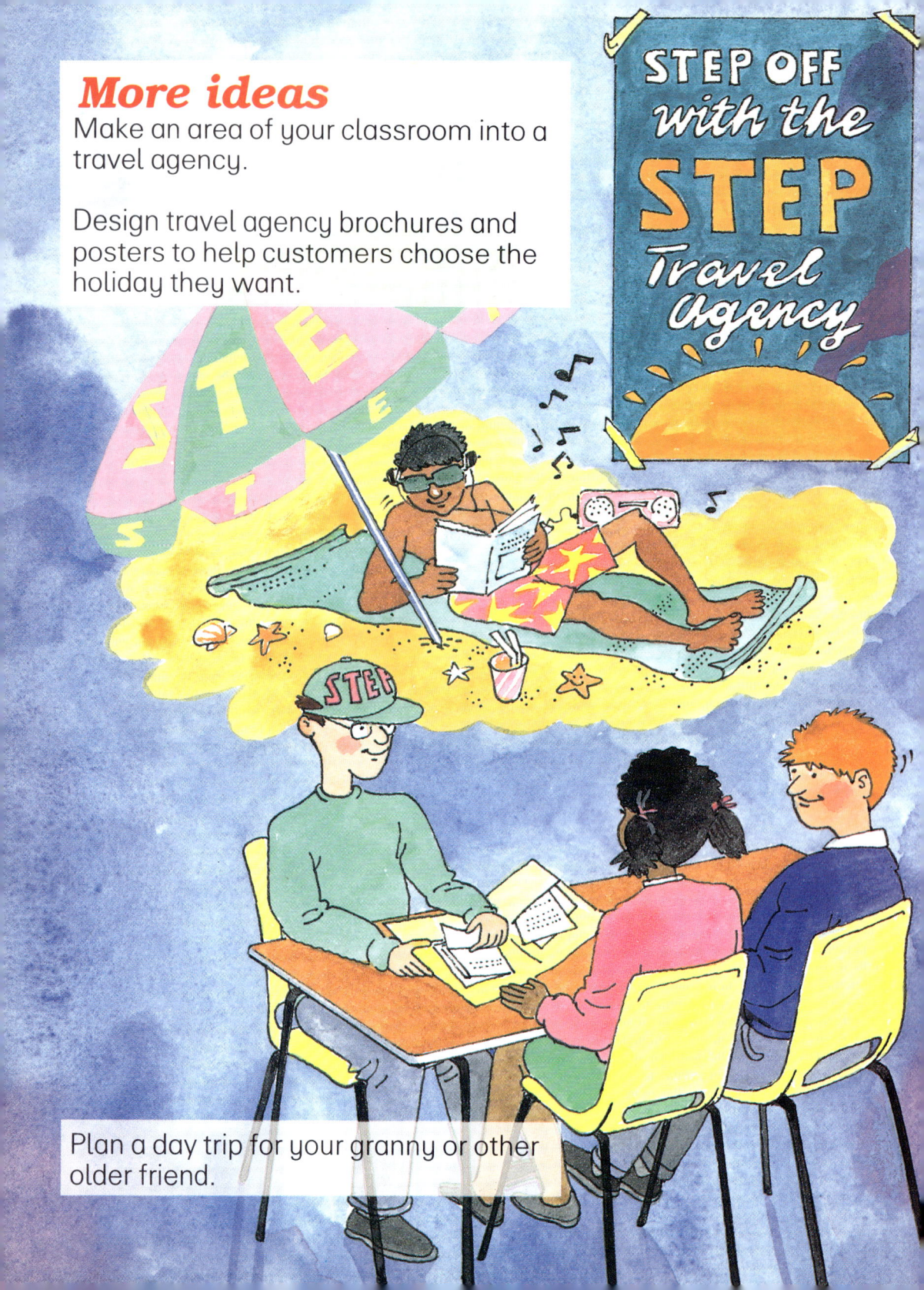

Make an area of your classroom into a travel agency.

Design travel agency brochures and posters to help customers choose the holiday they want.

STEP OFF with the STEP Travel Agency

Plan a day trip for your granny or other older friend.